MW01232350

Ynalogies

30 Devotions to Inspire Hope and Creativity

Written and illustrated by Yna Roa

Table of Analogies

FOR GRACEFULLY LOVING OTHERS

FOR EMBRACING GOD'S CREATIVE PROCESS AND PLAN

Dedication

To my father and brother in Heaven.
I love you with all my heart.

Introduction

Jesus spoke in parables. I like to speak in analogies—or Ynalogies, given my first name. I've been collecting these Ynalogies-of-life over the years, never quite sure what I would do with them, until God challenged me to craft them into a devotional.

I decided to illustrate this devotional because who doesn't love a good visual? Now, not to be overly modest, but these are rather simple visuals that are mediocre on an artistic level. The pictures are all comprised of the only thing I know how to draw: Triangles.

My artistic interest in triangles goes back to an evening I spent on the floor of my best friend's apartment. She had invited me over for an art night. She is a wildly talented artist who studied fashion for her major. She was updating me on her life, and we were having a very deep discussion as we drew.

My friend was sketching a beautiful floral skeleton-woman on the back of a rose-gold spray-painted skateboard. Meanwhile, I was hunched over in the cramped corner of the room drawing basic triangles. I felt so unqualified.

I often felt the same way while working on this book. Why on Earth would I write a devotional? In these moments of low self-confidence, I'm learning God loves to use unqualified people to do His work.

When I was in middle school geometry class, I remember a time when I first learned the properties of triangles. My dad helped me with my homework that evening. He told me that all the angles of a triangle add up to 180 degrees. I passionately disagreed with him. My father, who had studied engineering, insisted that was a rule. But I, a sassy seventh grader, was sure I knew better.

Acting on my pride, I drew a triangle and whipped out my protractor to measure its angles.

"See, dad? The angles only added up to 178 degrees! *It's two degrees short!* You're wrong!"

My dad stared at me and half smiled. He patiently and softly replied, "Yna, look at your book."

He showed me the rule clearly bolded in my textbook stating the angles of a triangle do indeed add up to 180 degrees.

Just as I argued with my father as a child, I argued with God when He urged me to create this piece of work. He was wrong about me, I was sure.

"God, I'm unqualified. I'm not enough. Like Moses, I am not eloquent of speech. No one cares. Why would anyone want to read this? It looks so childish! God, I am *two degrees short* from perfect in creating this devotional."

Again, like my earthly father had done, I picture my Heavenly Father patiently smiling back at me showing me His textbook of life.

"Not that we are competent in ourselves to claim anything
for ourselves, but our competence comes from God."
—2 Corinthians 3:5 (NIV)

Such a simple rule.

My hope for you is to be inspired as you read these devotionals. I hope that your mindset is reframed a little if you're feeling spiritually stuck. Let creativity take over.

Contrary to typical devotionals, these devotionals are not meant to be read in a specific order. Yes, I broke them down into categories, but you should read them in an order that speaks to you in your current walk with Jesus. There are also *spiritual challenges* I added as optional material. I understand the challenges might not be applicable for everyone, but keep an open mind! We grow the most when we step out of our comfort zone.

I pray that you may be inspired to do what God has called you to do in life. If you are a little lost and don't know what that purpose is, then I pray that God reveals a little bit of His plans to you. Let us push past the pain to create what God wants of us for His glory and to further His kingdom.

I've lived through a painful life full of many trials, as I'm sure we all have. I just want to be able to show you that God can take pain and create something beautiful. Through all of this, there is just one thing I want you to know: *You are so dearly loved by your Creator.*

For the Lost

Part 1

Wind

I was all set to start with my first analogy. "Life is like the wind," I wrote, "always changing and blowing us in different directions." But then, as if to prove my point, the Lord changed my heart and direction of where He wanted this analogy to go.

I grew up in Los Angeles where the Santa Ana winds would billow and howl very harshly at times. One year when I was very young, the wind blew so fiercely it knocked out the power of my house. I was terrified! The house shook and rumbled, the lights were out, and I had no sense of safety. My instincts kicked in, and I ran to my source of comfort. I ran to my dad, and I hugged him ever so tightly. We were in the middle of the living room just embracing each other. We stood there for a while until I calmed down. He was a source of comfort for me in the darkness.

Reflecting on that situation, I am reminded of the Gospel story of when Jesus was out on a boat with His disciples during a storm. The strong wind and choppy waters threatened to sink the boat. In their panic, the disciples called out to Jesus.

"And they went and woke him, saying, 'Save us, Lord; we are perishing.' And he said to them, 'Why are you afraid, O you of little faith?' Then he rose and rebuked the winds and the sea, and there was a great calm. And the men marveled, saying, 'What sort of man is this, that even winds and sea obey him?'"
—Matthew 8:23–27 (ESV)

Life releases gusts of wind. Our lives aren't always calm and peaceful, but we must trust in the Lord; He will calm the storm. If you are ever afraid, run to Jesus.

Verses

"Then they cried out to the Lord in their trouble, and he brought them out of their distress. He stilled the storm to a whisper; the waves of the sea were hushed. They were glad when it grew calm,

and he guided them to their desired haven. Let them give thanks to the Lord for his unfailing love and his wonderful deeds for mankind." —Psalm 107:28-31 (NIV)

"Who is like you, Lord God Almighty? You, Lord, are mighty, and your faithfulness surrounds you. You rule over the surging sea; when its waves mount up, you still them." —Psalm 89:8-9 (NIV)

Prayer

Father God, thank You for guiding me and keeping me safe during the storms of life. May I continue to focus my eyes on You whenever life gets difficult.

Spiritual Challenge

If you notice that a storm in your life is approaching, turn to Jesus. Take a moment and picture yourself on the boat with Jesus. Remember where you are and who you are with.

Notes

When I first moved to Massachusetts, I didn't know anything about the area. My new roommate invited me to go to the beach one sunny day, since I had never been to a beach on the East Coast.

When we arrived at the beach, my roommate took out a kite from her bag. Being well into my twenties, I had not flown a kite in a long time. I forgot how exhilarating it was to fly a kite. Exhilarating and, in this case, exhausting. The wind was not very strong that day, so I had to run up and down the beach to generate my own wind.

Our life in Christ is like a kite. We must stay grounded in the Word and with God. And we must maintain a good balance of teamwork for we are part of the body of Christ.

God has created me to be very imaginative, and I tend to try to navigate life on my own, but I must rely on God to ground me. If not, I will be like a kite without a string, and I will crash eventually.

"Trust in the Lord with all your heart and lean not on your own understanding; in all your ways submit to him, and he will make your paths straight." —Proverbs 3:5-6 (NIV)

A kite suspended in midair is strikingly beautiful. People all around will turn their heads and stare. What we do for God's glory will catch people's attention.

"In the same way, let your light shine before others, that they may see your good deeds and glorify your Father in heaven."
—Matthew 5:16 (NIV)

Additionally, flying a kite is a very youthful experience. We are told in the Bible to approach the Kingdom with childlike faith.

"And he said: 'Truly I tell you, unless you change and become like little children, you will never enter the kingdom of heaven.'"
—Matthew 18:3 (NIV)

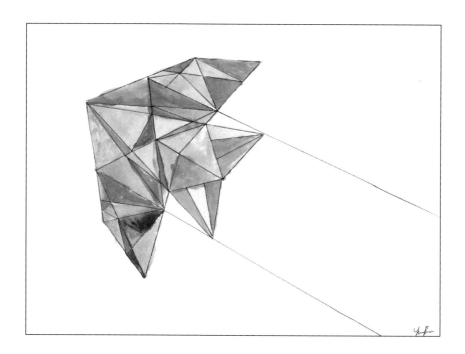

Verses

(In the entry)

Prayer

Father God, I thank You for this exhilarating journey that we are on together. May I continue to work on what You have called me to do with complete joy. Please ground me in the Word and inspire me through it.

Spiritual Challenge

Go fly a kite! (If that isn't a good option where you live, pick a different creative activity.) God gave us all talents and skills. Sometimes we can get burdened with always trying to find a way to produce something effective—and we forget to have fun. You never know what God will say to you or how He will inspire you when you are in a joyful state of fun.

Notes

_____

_____

_____

_____

_____

_____

_____

_____

_____

_____

_____

_____

_____

_____

_____

_____

_____

_____

Pilot Light

Do you realize the significance of a pilot light? It is a small light hidden underneath a water heater, usually placed somewhere inconspicuous. The water heater in my house is located outdoors, so whenever it rains really hard or the wind blows, the pilot light goes out. We usually can't tell at first. But the water in the house gets cold slowly over time until there is no more hot water left.

It is such a tricky process to strike up the pilot light again! You have to turn off the gas and wait a little bit. Then you turn the knob to "pilot" and push the button on the side while you hit the strike button until the pilot light is lit. It can take a few tries.

Sometimes our souls can turn a little cold. The light gets knocked out of us by our circumstances. We can lose our light instantaneously in one tragic moment, or the light can fade gradually over time. However, there is hope. We have Jesus. He can help us reignite the fire in our soul.

We all need hope and inspiration. Without hope, it feels like God is distant. We feel a little bit colder and a little bit off. But once the spark is relit in us, we are unstoppable. Once we have that inspired connection with God, we can do all things through Christ.

If your light is out, be sure to have compassion for yourself. Yes, sometimes we mess up, but our lack of zeal isn't always our fault! There is an Enemy out there, so have compassion, dear one. Don't put too much focus on why the light went out—focus on how to fire it up again!

Verses

"Never be lacking in zeal, but keep your spiritual fervor,
serving the Lord. Be joyful in hope, patient in affliction,
faithful in prayer." —Romans 12:11–12 (NIV)

"They asked each other, 'Were not our hearts burning within us while he talked with us on the road and opened the Scriptures to us?'" —Luke 24:32 (NIV)

Prayer

Father God, I pray that You would divinely inspire me. Set a fire in my soul so I may go out into the world on Your behalf. Thank You for always encouraging me and for not giving up on me.

Spiritual Challenge

Do something that sparks joy and inspires you today.

Notes

_____

_____

_____

_____

_____

_____

_____

_____

_____

_____

_____

_____

_____

_____

_____

_____

_____

_____

_____

Treasure Map

Life can be like a search for buried treasure. Sometimes God feels just as distant as that buried treasure, but the frustration we feel compels us to keep digging. Whenever I am frustrated, confused, lost or upset over something prominent in my mind, I use it as an invitation to lean into God.

When lost, we can discern our direction by following a map. My soul is desperate to follow the treasure map to the solution to my problem, and what I'm looking for is always found in the Word and Jesus. However, the route to peace looks different each time. If I'm angry, I read verses on anger and stories of people in the Bible who dealt with anger. I also ask my trusted community of people how they deal with anger.

Usually if I'm in the middle of a frustrating situation, this means I have an opportunity to grow closer to God. Through the process, I am slowly becoming the person God is molding me to be. When I follow God's leading and reach the end of the map, the hidden treasure is the lesson I learned. This treasure adds tremendous value to my life. Of course, the valuable treasure I acquired is meant to be shared with people, so I seek to help others find their way whenever I am given the opportunity.

Verses

"May he give you the desire of your heart and make all your plans succeed." —Psalm 20:4 (NIV)

"For where your treasure is, there your heart will be also." —Matthew 6:1 (NIV)

"The kingdom of heaven is like treasure hidden in a field. When a man found it, he hid it again, and then in his joy went and sold all he had and bought that field." —Matthew 13:44 (NIV)

Prayer

Dear Heavenly Father, as frustrating as life can be, I thank You for the opportunity to turn the difficult situations into a way to grow closer to You. I pray for guidance as I navigate through such difficult moments, and I pray that I am able to help people who are going through similar situations. Inspire us all with hope, Father God.

Spiritual Challenge

If you are frustrated about something in your life, find a character in the Bible who went through something similar. Find the treasure in their story.

Notes

Slack-line

I remember when I first stepped foot on a slack-line in college. Someone had tied one between two trees just outside of our dining hall. One by one, students walked up and conquered this slack-line with ease.

Wow, that's so cool! They make it seem so easy! But I don't think I have enough core strength for this...

Nonetheless, with much encouragement from my peers, I decided to try it out. After much fumbling, I finally got on the line and—did I cross the line?

Nope!

I kind of just stood there for a second, took a few steps, lost my balance, and instinctively jumped off before I could face-plant on the ground.

Was I ever able to complete it?

Nope!

I wish I had an awesome testimony of how God gave me superhuman core strength and helped me conquer such a feat for His glory, but no, that was not the case. However, God still gets the glory for the spiritual lessons I learned from the 2.5 seconds I was able to stay upright on such a thin line of material.

What did I learn? Life is a balancing act.

Should we act or react? Are we supposed to wait for a clear sign from God or do we just take a leap of faith? Should we follow God's command to *Be still and know that I am God* or *Get up, pick up your mat, and walk?* What do we do?

For starters, we need to fix our eyes on Jesus.

When I first hoisted myself onto the slack-line, I had to keep my eyes focused on something in order to keep my balance. Conveniently, there was an affixed wooden cross on one of the trees that I was able to fix my gaze upon.

We must keep our eyes on Jesus during our journey.

It is a constant balancing act, but as long as we keep our focus on Jesus and keep walking toward Him, He will be able to get us through the journey. We might not get through it gracefully, we might take forever to cross, we might have to pick ourselves off the ground a few times, but God will get us through.

If you're trying to make a decision, don't be afraid to take a chance and jump on that slack-line journey. Maybe you've been watching from the sidelines. Or perhaps you're on the ground after a failed attempt to do it on your own, wondering if you should give up. Don't get caught up in analysis paralysis; just jump on the line. If you lean too much to one side and fall off, that's okay. God's grace will get you back up again. Just remember to focus on Jesus.

Verses

"Fixing our eyes on Jesus, the pioneer and perfecter of faith. For the joy set before him he endured the cross, scorning its shame, and sat down at the right hand of the throne of God." —Hebrews 12:2 (NIV)

"Walk in obedience to all that the Lord your God has commanded you, so that you may live and prosper and prolong your days in the land that you will possess." —Deuteronomy 5:33 (NIV)

"Jesus answered, 'I am the way and the truth and the life. No one comes to the Father except through me.'" —John 14:6 (NIV)

Prayer

Dear Jesus, help me to fix my eyes on You always. In this season of life, let me see You clearly and follow You confidently. Thank You for guiding me thus far.

Spiritual Challenge

If you are unsure of where to go or what to do, seek Jesus. Whenever I am stuck in life, I look to people in the Bible and see if their journey is applicable to what I am going through today.

Notes

Desert

Life is like the desert. There are moments in which I feel spiritually dry. In these moments, I am tempted to turn toward worldly things to fill my soul. But I must remember that these are mirages.

I admire the life that thrives in extreme climates. Even though life is less abundant in the desert, it is still home to many plants, animals, and other creatures. We too can find nourishment within the spiritual deserts we must pass through on occasion.

Gratitude gets me through the dry seasons of life. The discovery of any form of life helps me press on when I am lost and tired. When I acknowledge the little blessings God has given me even in my desert season, I am sustained.

Without fail, when I reach the little oasis in the desert and God refills my soul, the moment is so precious to me because I have been deprived of life-giving water for so long. My soul rejoices greatly when I have been greatly lacking. Look for God's faithfulness in harsh seasons of life, and remember to practice faithfulness.

Verses

"My soul thirsts for God, for the living God. When can I go and meet with God? My tears have been my food day and night, while people say to me all day long, 'Where is your God?' These things I remember as I pour out my soul: how I used to go to the house of God under the protection of the Mighty One with shouts of joy and praise among the festive throng." —Psalm 42:2-4 (NIV)

"You, God, are my God, earnestly I seek you; I thirst for you, my whole being longs for you, in a dry and parched land where there is no water. I have seen you in the sanctuary and beheld your power and your glory. Because your love is better than life, my lips will glorify you. I will praise you as long as I live, and in your name I will lift up my hands. I will be fully satisfied as with the richest of foods; with singing lips my mouth will praise you." —Psalm 63:1-5 (NIV)

*"Let everything that has breath praise the Lord.
Praise the Lord." —Psalm 150:6 (NIV)*

Prayer

Father God, thank You for never deserting me. My soul thirsts for You always. Renew my heart and soul, and walk with me through the seasons of spiritual dryness.

Spiritual Challenge

If you are going through a dry season of faith, I challenge you to practice gratitude and find something to be grateful for. Just like the little bit of life that thrives in the desert, there are good things to be grateful for in each day. Even the smallest cactus contributes life to the barren desert.

Notes

Frame

When you can't change your circumstances, reframe your mind in-stead with God's truth.

One of my creative classes in college was small enough to allow my professor to ask us individually, every week, to share something that reframed our mind. We would all go around and share some-thing significant about our week that caught our attention or forced us to change our perspective in some way. That exercise helped us listen to what everyone was going through and gave us the oppor-tunity to process our own experiences. I constantly think about that exercise, especially when my mental state is stuck on something and needs adjusting. Much like how a piece of art can have a different look once its frame is changed.

I personally struggle with jealousy. The intensity of these feel-ings has definitely subsided as I have grown up (thank You Jesus!), but I still get triggered on occasion. When this happens, I have to deliberately reframe my jealous thoughts as admiration. I tell my-self I am inspired by this person. When I look at her, I must see her as someone God created. I should admire her strengths and try to learn from them. I also make sure to keep a positive self-image, re-membering that my identity is in Christ and not my skills, looks, circumstances, or achievements.

Reframing my mind in this way helps diffuse the jealousy. I haven't perfected this technique, and I still get jealous from time to time. However, when I feel these emotions, I remember that I add value to the world because Jesus lives in me, and I try to reframe my mind according to this truth. I encourage you to try and do the same the next time you struggle with negative thoughts. Try to see your situation from a different perspective.

Verses

"We demolish arguments and every pretension that sets itself up against the knowledge of God, and we take captive every thought to make it obedient to Christ." —2 Corinthians 10:5 (NIV)

"Finally, brothers and sisters, whatever is true, whatever is noble, whatever is right, whatever is pure, whatever is lovely, whatever is admirable—if anything is excellent or praiseworthy—think about such things." —Philippians 4:8 (NIV)

Prayer

Father God, sometimes it is hard to understand the season You have me in. Help me to reframe my mind; please show me the good in all that is happening.

Spiritual Challenge

I challenge you to answer my professor's question: What reframed your mindset recently? Consider sharing this answer with someone around you.

Notes

Math Equation

Reading Scripture is like a math equation.

We learned several math formulas when I was in school. We would even sing songs to help us memorize the formulas. During testing time, if you glanced around, you would see people subtly singing to themselves.

In class we would learn the formulas, and then our teacher would break down each one and show us how to apply it. We learned the subject material with the understanding that it would be on a test.

Scripture is like this. I sometimes read the Bible and cannot comprehend it at first, so I have to keep studying. I can learn about the context of when it was written. I can ask pastors for their interpretation. I can pray and ask God for insight. And finally, I need to apply it. We are sometimes tested in life. When put to the test, does the perfect scriptural insight pop into our head or do we draw a blank? If nothing comes to mind right away, don't give up! In school we would get partial credit for attempted answers on tests, but we never got any points if we didn't try at all.

Sometimes you may read a Bible passage and have no idea what its application could be. You might not know in the moment why you need that piece of Scripture, but eventually, during a test of life, you'll find it easier to reframe your mind (not your circumstances) with Scripture. It can help carry you through the difficult time.

If you're struggling with a math equation and come testing time don't know how to solve a problem, you might be staring at the page for a really long time; you might try to use other methods to solve the equation; or if you're desperate, you might try to cheat.

When in the middle of a crisis, sometimes we rely on our past hurt in a cynical way instead of looking for God's help. We might just be stuck for a really long time in a situation, or we might cheat in life and try to use other people to get to where we want to be.

As difficult as it might be to study God's textbook, it will help you out in the end and guide you through tests of life.

Verses

"Keep this Book of the Law always on your lips; meditate on it day and night, so that you may be careful to do everything written in it. Then you will be prosperous and successful." —Joshua 1:8 (NIV)

"He read it aloud from daybreak till noon as he faced the square before the Water Gate in the presence of the men, women and others who could understand. And all the people listened attentively to the Book of the Law." —Nehemiah 8:3 (NIV)

"Consequently, faith comes from hearing the message, and the message is heard through the word about Christ." —Romans 10:17 (NIV)

"For the word of God is alive and active. Sharper than any double-edged sword, it penetrates even to dividing soul and spirit, joints and marrow; it judges the thoughts and attitudes of the heart." —Hebrews 4:12 (NIV)

"All Scripture is God-breathed and is useful for teaching, rebuking, correcting and training in righteousness, so that the servant of God may be thoroughly equipped for every good work." —2 Timothy 3:16–17 (NIV)

"I have hidden your word in my heart that I might not sin against you." —Psalm 119:11 (NIV)

Prayer

Father God, thank You for providing me Scripture to live by to help me through difficult times. Help me to fully comprehend what You are trying to tell me through Scripture. I pray that whenever there is a difficult moment in life, I will be able to lean on Your Word to get me through.

Spiritual Challenge

Memorize three verses of Scripture. Verses that ring true to you. Not only will these verses help you face future adversity, you never know when you might need to encourage someone else later on.

(I'll give you a gold star!)

Notes

Violin

*When I was in elementary school, I remember my first orchestra con-*cert very distinctly. I stood up to go to the bathroom before the concert commenced. As I was getting up, I tripped over my music stand and sat on my violin! I looked down and saw the bow and shoulder rest had both snapped in half. I started to panic.

I immediately ran to my teacher and told her what happened. She miraculously whipped out a spare bow from the closet, and I got to play after all (it was just a little uncomfortable without a shoulder rest). My teacher modeled how God comes to our aid when we need help. He provides for us when we need something if we are willing to go to Him (see Philippians 4:19).

Like a violin, our souls must be kept in tune. When violins are off-pitch, they cannot be played properly. People born with perfect pitch will know immediately when their instrument is out of tune, but most of us are relative pitch learners. We must train ourselves to hear when our instrument is out of tune.

We must re-tune our souls or else we might be performing off key. When we are slightly off, spiritually or mentally, it's nothing to be ashamed of. It means we are human. An instrument gets out of tune if you play a lot, or if it has been sitting in the closet for a while—or if you manage to sit on it as I did! We need time to re-tune ourselves and make sure our lives are glorifying God.

We can tune ourselves by reading the Word and focusing on God's truth instead of listening to the sound of lies. We can train our spiritual ears to recognize when we are out of tune by reading God's Word. Another method of tuning our souls is taking time to pray as Jesus did. Jesus often withdrew from the crowds and spent time praying by himself. His model is a great example of how we can realign and re-tune ourselves.

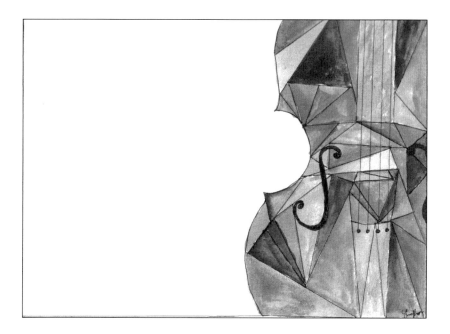

Verses

"But Jesus often withdrew to lonely places and prayed."
—Luke 5:16 (NIV)

"A good man brings good things out of the good stored up in his heart, and an evil man brings evil things out of the evil stored up in his heart. For the mouth speaks what the heart is full of."
—*Luke 6:45 (NIV)*

"Do not harden your hearts as you did in the rebellion, during the time of testing in the wilderness."
—*Hebrews 3:8 (NIV)*

"And my God will meet all your needs according to the riches of his glory in Christ Jesus." —Philippians 4:19 (NIV)

Prayer

Father God, I pray that You tune my soul whenever I am feeling off. Let me rest and abide in You and meditate on Your word. Thank you for all that You do.

Spiritual Challenge

Take some time out of your day to re-tune yourself. Pray to God and spend time with Him! (Bonus challenge: if you play an instrument, go pick it up and practice!)

Notes

For the Broken

Part 2

Stained Glass Window

Loss seems to be a common occurrence in my life, unfortunately. I lost my brother when I was eleven, and a decade later I lost my father. Two very important and special guys in my life are no longer here on Earth.

Their absence broke me. I tried to hide my brokenness. I masked it with humor and smiles, but internally I was a mess. I had to actively keep surrendering my pain to God; only then was I able to find healing.

I wrote this poem about the losses I have experienced in my life and how the loss affected me. It was written during a painful yet inspiring season. I'm sharing it here just to show how God can turn something broken into something beautiful.

If you feel broken, I encourage you to surrender to God. Let Him work on your heart and soul. You will get through this; embrace the journey.

Poem

Glass

I was a glass vase
I kept flowers in place
I held things that were pretty
Until one day I fell, and life got gritty

I was put together again with grace
But I was never quite the same vase
If you looked close you would see
The little lines of brokenness there would be

Therefore I hid myself from view
I didn't want my brokenness to shine through
I lived like this for many years
The leaking water being my tears

I thought I would not have more pain to endure
Nothing worse could happen, I was sure
But life decided to knock me down once more
Again, I was left shattered on the floor

This time, I laid there untouched
To the broken pieces of myself, I clutched
Instead of rushing to get back up once more
I decided I should leave the pieces on the floor

While time began to pass
My creator took the broken glass

And slowly mended the pieces into something new
Something that couldn't be hidden from view

I wasn't going to be the same glass vase
I had no idea what, but the journey, I would embrace
In the end I was made anew
I became a stained-glass window, in plain view

No more hiding anymore
No more lying on the floor
I was a glass vase
But that is no longer the case

-Yna Roa

Verses

"And the God of all grace, who called you to his eternal glory in Christ, after you have suffered a little while, will himself restore you and make you strong, firm and steadfast." —1 Peter 5:10 (NIV)

"Heal me, Lord, and I will be healed; save me and I will be saved, for you are the one I praise." —Jeremiah 17:14 (NIV)

Prayer

Father God, I pray for peace and comfort during times of pain. Take my pain, and one day allow me to help someone else. Thank You for holding me close, and thank You for mending my broken heart.

Spiritual Challenge

This challenge is more of a long-term challenge. I challenge you to let God work in your life. To let go of leaning on your own understanding, and to hold onto Him throughout the difficult seasons in your life. Writing is cathartic to me; I encourage you to find your outlet and pour yourself into it.

Notes

Bonsai Tree

People are like bonsai trees. Bonsai trees are cultivated into minia-ture versions of full-grown trees through constant, painstaking pruning. Perhaps you are currently in a painful pruning season; if so, take heart. Your spirit is being pruned so that you may be shaped into a beautiful creation. God is merely getting rid of the parts of your spirit that are hurting you more than helping you.

Even Jesus went through suffering and pruning:

"During the days of Jesus' life on earth, he offered up prayers and petitions with fervent cries and tears to the one who could save him from death, and he was heard because of his reverent submission. Son though he was, he learned obedience from what he suffered."
—Hebrews 5:7–8 (NIV)

Once a bonsai tree is brought to its intended shape, it doesn't stop needing to be nurtured. An unknown writer once said, "Bonsai is not a race, nor is it a destination. It is a never-ending journey."

Life is not about arrival or success—it's about the journey. God wants to walk with you throughout your journey.

Verses

"He cuts off every branch in me that bears no fruit, while every branch that does bear fruit he prunes so that it will be even more fruitful. You are already clean because of the word I have spoken to you. Remain in me, as I also remain in you. No branch can bear fruit by itself; it must remain in the vine. Neither can you bear fruit unless you remain in me." –John 15:2-4 (NIV)

"Consider it pure joy, my brothers and sisters, whenever you face trials of many kinds, because you know that the testing of your faith produces perseverance. Let perseverance finish its work so that you may be mature and complete, not lacking anything. If any

of you lacks wisdom, you should ask God, who gives generously
to all without finding fault, and it will be given to you."
—James 1:2-5 (NIV)

Prayer

Dear Heavenly Father, I pray that You would cut off all of the parts of my soul that are causing me more harm than good. Nurture me, shape me, mold me to be more like Christ.

Spiritual Challenge

Reflect on what you think God is working on in you. If you are internally struggling with something unpleasant, give it to God and see how He handles it. This might be a painful pruning season, but the end results will cause you to flourish.

Notes

Splinter

When I was a young child, I once went to the hardware store with my dad. I sat in the cart as he purchased wood for some project for the house.

My curiosity and childish impulse randomly led me to stick my little finger in between two pieces of wood. When I pulled my finger out, it was covered with painful splinters! I started bawling in the middle of the store.

My dad saw what I had done and immediately swooped me up in his arms, left the cart full of products in the middle of the aisle, and ran to the car where he had a first-aid kit.

We were in the parking lot for a long time, while my dad diligently pulled out every single splinter. One by one. I was crying and in pain.

Looking back, I'm grateful and amazed that my father never berated me for doing something foolish or acting on my curiosity. He just wanted to take the pain away. He wasn't in a rush, and he dropped everything to take care of me.

God blessed me with a father who modeled my Heavenly Father so well. Through my father's actions in this painful situation, I have been given a great example of how God works in the lives of His children.

Little Yna can be compared to an accidental sinner. I didn't know any better when I put my hand where it didn't belong, and often we sin without realizing what we're doing. God sees that we are in pain and comes to our rescue. We don't notice everything He does for us because we are too busy crying. He sacrifices everything to help us.

If you need God, it is okay to lament. The Psalms are full of praise and lamentation. My father heard me cry and helped me out; in the same way, God hears our cries and comes to our aid.

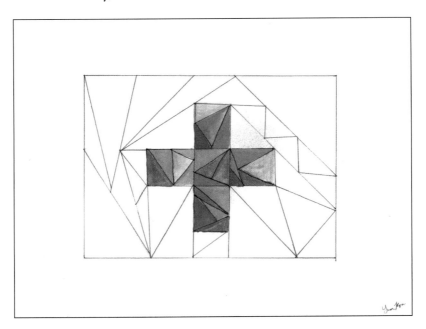

Verses

"In my distress I called to the Lord; I called out to my God.
From his temple he heard my voice; my cry came to his ears."
—2 Samuel 22:7 (NIV)

"He heals the brokenhearted and binds up their wounds."
—Psalm 147:3 (NIV)

Prayer

Dear Heavenly Father, as life continues to cause pain, may I run to You for comfort and healing. Thank You for Your kindness and patience.

Spiritual Challenge

Practice compassion for yourself today. Sometimes life can get really difficult both internally and externally. If you are hurting, ask God to help you. If you are in pain, pray to God.

Notes

Ice Skating

When I was in preschool, I told everyone I wanted to be a professional ice skater. My dream quickly died when I realized that ice skating takes skill, hard work, balance, money, practice, and a lot of falls.

I haven't stepped on an ice rink that often in my life, but there was one memorable occasion with my trek group in Yosemite. Our leader saw a frozen pond and tested it out to see if we would be able to skate on it. The ice held, and we had so much fun skating around and spending quality time with each other.

Skating on ice is much like our journey with Jesus. If you're going to stumble (and sin), you might as well stumble in the presence of the Lord. I'm not suggesting you sin on purpose, but when it happens, don't let shame keep you from enjoying fellowship with God and your community. We all fall short. Might as well stumble in God's rink.

Ice skaters fall. They don't intend to fall. Their intent is to leap high and be graceful while landing, but falling happens sometimes. Even when we take a leap of faith, we might still fall. Just be resilient, and trust that the Lord will be there to help you back to your feet.

Like preschool me with my ice skating dreams, we all have ideas about what our journey with Jesus will look like, but reality will be different than what we expect. I thought I was going to be a professional ice skater with sparkly outfits, medals, glory, and crowds of people throwing flowers at me. Nope.

However, I still was able to ice skate in Yosemite. It just was a different context. Skating that day was even better than the professional ice skater fantasy I dreamed of. I got to enjoy quality time in God's creation with good friends.

I believe this is how Jesus wants to spend time with us. He wants us to be in community with Him. Trusting Him that He will be there when we fall.

Verses

"The Lord makes firm the steps of the one who delights in him; though he may stumble, he will not fall, for the Lord upholds him with his hand." —Psalm 37:23-24 (NIV)

"For all have sinned and fall short of the glory of God, and all are justified freely by his grace through the redemption that came by Christ Jesus." —Romans 3:23-24 (NIV)

Prayer

Father God, bestow an overwhelming sense of grace and compassion over me in times when I feel discouraged for stumbling. Thank You for catching me when I fall.

Spiritual Challenge

Have you "failed" at something lately? Ask God to help you through the discouragement. I also challenge you to think of *two times* that you succeeded at something lately—even if they were small victories! I believe that counteracting that one negative incident with two positive ones is a victory in itself.

Notes

Diamond

Every time I'm in a difficult season, I hold onto the fact that I am being shaped like a diamond. I just got out of a dark season recently, a season of apathy and distance from God. Although I felt this way, I chose to believe that He was shaping me.

Diamonds are formed deep in the dark soil under high-pressure environments. Diamond formation takes time and isolation, and their retrieval requires deep excavation. These rare items are optimally formed in nature. It is possible to synthesize a diamond, and the process is indeed faster, but it's imperfect: air pockets are formed in synthetic diamonds.

This is reflective of human work versus God's work. Yes, we can be shaped by the people around us, but God can fashion us into something far more beautiful and pure.

You are so precious and valuable. If you are in a difficult and dark season, hold on to God's promises of hope.

Verses

"In all this you greatly rejoice, though now for a little while
you may have had to suffer grief in all kinds of trials.
These have come so that the proven genuineness of your faith—
of greater worth than gold, which perishes even though refined
by fire—may result in praise, glory and honor when Jesus Christ is
revealed. Though you have not seen him, you love him; and
even though you do not see him now, you believe in him
and are filled with an inexpressible and glorious joy, for
you are receiving the end result of your faith, the salvation
of your souls."—1 Peter 1:6-9 (NIV)

"See, I have refined you, though not as silver; I have tested
you in the furnace of affliction."—Isaiah 48:10 (NIV)

Prayer

Dear Heavenly Father, continue to mold and shape me during times of trouble. Please hold me close and protect me from life's afflictions.

Spiritual Challenge

If you are going through a dark season, I challenge you to choose to believe God is shaping you. That's it. No action required; just trust God.

Notes

Ynalogies

Illustrations by Yna Roa
Cover design by Erik Peterson
Book design by Tobi Carter

ISBN 978-0-578-67890-0 (paperback)
ISBN 978-0-578-68284-6 (ebook)

For more information, visit https://ynalogies.com
or email ynaroa@ynalogies.com

Baking

One time in high school, my friend threw a themed marathon party in honor of a new young adult book-turned-movie coming out. You might be familiar with it. It involves vampires and werewolves. Anyway, I wanted to contribute something to the party, so I decided to bake cake pops.

I had never made cake pops before, but the process is actually very interesting. You first have to bake a cake fully and then crumble it into a bowl. The next step is to add frosting and roll the mixture into balls. Then stick them in the fridge. Once cooled, you dip them in chocolate, and they are pretty much done.

Later in college, I attempted a similar recipe but with cheesecake instead. It failed miserably. To cover my mistake, I drizzled the lumps of cheesecake in chocolate and called them "Yna's famously flawed cheesecake bites." I fed them to my hungry and broke college roommates. They loved it! Even my lactose-intolerant friends powered through them with delight!

Your stomach is probably growling now, huh? While I can't fill your empty stomach right now—unless you eat the pages of the book—at the very least, I hope I can fill your spiritual cravings with this analogy.

There have been so many times when I felt like I crumbled under pressure. The weight of the world seemed too heavy. I begged God to take that thorn from my side. Oftentimes it felt like He didn't help at all—or perhaps not in the way I imagined.

God challenges us to rise above the current circumstances and trust that even though the process will be messy, we'll be alright in the end. Your particular situation might end up the way you want, or it might not at all. However, it is important to savor the journey and the process. God will take the mess-ups and the failures and make something enjoyable from them—something we can share with the world.

Even if our journeys and testimonies are not the most presentable or profound, this doesn't mean people won't benefit from what we have to say. Like I mentioned before, even my lactose-intolerant friends enjoyed my cheesecake bites! Share your story; share your pain. Others will love hearing what you have to say, even if it might be difficult to ingest and digest. Your story matters.

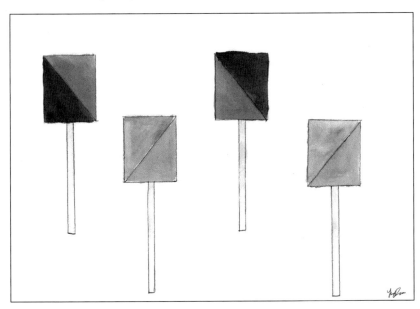

Verses

"Jesus did not let him, but said, 'Go home to your own people and tell them how much the Lord has done for you, and how he has had mercy on you.'" —Mark 5:19 (NIV)

"For we are God's handiwork, created in Christ Jesus to do good works, which God prepared in advance for us to do." —Ephesians 2:10 (NIV)

Prayer

Dear Heavenly Father, I pray that You would take my failures and mess-ups and turn them into something great for Your glory. Let me help others along the way as well.

Spiritual Challenge

Bake something! As you do, think about how God has worked in your life. Then share what you baked with someone, along with your testimony. You could also just share your testimony, but I figured it would be a bonus to bake something sweet for someone sweet!

Notes

Pearl

You are a pearl. You are precious. You are fearfully and wonderfully made.

Pearls are made from a speck of sand agitating the inside of a mollusk, clam, or oyster. Have you ever looked at a clam or a mollusk? They are really quite ugly from the exterior—or unappealing might be a nicer word. Someone out there might strongly disagree with me and claim that clams are the most beautiful creations on the planet, and I respect that.

Most people overlook clams because they look plain from the outside. Nevertheless, they contain something very precious inside. They contain pearls. People even go out of their way and dive deep to retrieve such precious pearls. The Australian silver-lipped oyster creates one of the rarest pearls in the world. The oyster lives in isolation at the bottom of the untouched sea, and the pearls take years to form.

You must see yourself as a beautiful pearl. Even if you might think you are culturally unattractive or worthless, *you are precious. You are valuable. You are rare.* Repeat this to yourself always. You add value to the world. The world is missing out if you hide behind a hard shell. Unfortunately, people usually won't bother to try to see what's behind the shell. You must be willing to show people who you really are and who God made you to be.

Once you fully realize this, you'll be motivated to seek out other people's souls and let them know they are precious. People can act awfully. Those who seem to act hideous are just broken. Be willing to dive deep to help people retrieve their precious souls. Have mercy on people just as God has mercy on us. As we extend grace to others, we will get hurt and burnt out if we're drawing from our own capacity for mercy; our gift must spring from the love of God. We can help people retrieve their lost souls from the depths of the sorrowful sea with the help of Jesus.

Have empathy for people, not pity. Don't peer down at them from the top of the ocean in the safety of a boat—go down with them to the very bottom. But don't lean on yourself; if you simply take one breath, you won't last long under the sea. You will give up on people.

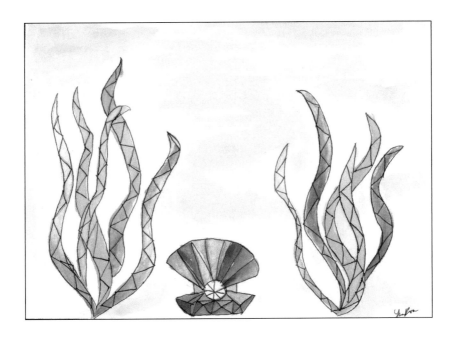

If you let Jesus sustain you instead, then you will be able to be with others during their pain.

Verses

"Then the Lord God formed a man from the dust of the ground and breathed into his nostrils the breath of life, and the man became a living being." —Genesis 2:7 (NIV)

"I praise you because I am fearfully and wonderfully made; your works are wonderful, I know that full well." —Psalm 139:14 (NIV)

"Your beauty should not come from outward adornment, such as elaborate hairstyles and the wearing of gold jewelry or fine clothes. Rather, it should be that of your inner self, the unfading beauty of a gentle and quiet spirit, which is of great worth in God's sight." —1 Peter 3:3-4 (NIV)

Prayer

Dear God, thank You for creating me in Your image. Help me to see myself as You see me. I also pray that I might see people the way You do and love them the way You want me to.

Spiritual Challenge

Say something positive about yourself, and understand your identity is in Christ. Then let someone know that they are valued too!

Notes

_____

_____

_____

_____

_____

_____

_____

_____

_____

_____

_____

_____

_____

_____

_____

_____

Manure

Yes, that's right. I said it. Life is like MANURE.

Once I was leading a missions trip without a set itinerary. A lot of people dropped out at the last minute, and everything just seemed like a mess. Thankfully, the missions team came up with the idea of beautifying our host church and planting a new garden for the incoming pastor. The week started off rocky, but ended up being impactful.

That gardening project introduced me to manure, which is literally animal feces mixed with straw. Added to soil, it helps plants grow. It is nutrient rich, even though the concept is a little off-putting.

God wants to use the messy, chaotic situations in life and turn them into opportunities for amazing growth.

There are daily struggles that we all go through. These difficult situations will seem less painful if we give them to God. Let Him take our mess and allow something beautiful to grow from it.

Verses

"Behold, God is my helper; the Lord is the upholder of my life."
—Psalm 54:4 (ESV)

"For our light and momentary troubles are achieving for us
an eternal glory that far outweighs them all."
—2 Corinthians 4:17 (NIV)

Prayer

Father God, I let go of all the negative situations of my life in hopes that You will turn it into something beautiful. Let me grow as a person from adversity. I lean on You during this difficult growing season.

Spiritual Challenge

If you are having a day that is unpleasant and full of manure, I challenge you to try to make someone else's day. Tell someone a joke, give someone flowers, or simply smile! It creates a joyful moment out of a place of sadness.

Notes

_____

_____

_____

_____

_____

_____

_____

_____

_____

_____

_____

_____

_____

_____

_____

_____

_____

_____

For Gracefully Loving Others

Part 3

Bee

People are like bees. Sweet like honey, but ready to sting you when they feel their world is threatened.

I used to get stung by bees a lot as a child. When I was three, I distinctly remember sitting in my stroller admiring various animals at the zoo. I was innocently sitting there when a bee decided to land on my knee and sting me! I was so shocked at this sudden sting of pain that my natural instinct was to cry.

My dad's natural instinct was to protect his child. He immediately pulled out the stinger and scrambled to put ice on my little swollen knee. As I was crying, I questioned why something would inflict pain on me when all I was doing was just sitting there.

However, looking at the nature of bees, the reason they sting is merely for protection. When a honeybee stings a person, the stinger breaks off—along with part of the bee's abdomen. The bee does not survive. Yet bees will use this defense mechanism anyway to protect their world when they feel threatened.

People are like this. People will lash out when frightened or insecure. If they have an unstable environment, they may mistake your well-intentioned interaction for an intrusion.

Don't worry. As long as you trust God and understand His truth that You are His child, He will pull out the stinger and place ice on your wound.

But bees also serve a positive purpose. They pollinate flowers and produce honey; they are good creatures! People can also be naturally sweet and caring too!

Weaving this analogy into the Bible, Joseph was stung by his own brothers. They betrayed him out of jealousy merely because he was being himself. Merely because he was expressing the dreams that God gave him. They betrayed him and sold him to the Ishmaelites, but God took out their stingers and made an incredible story out of Joseph's pain.

[just bee yourself!]

Verses

"Gracious words are a honeycomb, sweet to the soul and healing to the bones." —Proverbs 16:24 (NIV)

"But Joseph said to them, 'Don't be afraid. Am I in the place of God? You intended to harm me, but God intended it for good to accomplish what is now being done, the saving of many lives.'" —Genesis 50:19-20 (NIV)

Prayer

Father God, I thank You for protecting me and guarding my heart. Help me to forgive those who have hurt me, and I ask forgiveness for hurting others. May my community work together as a whole to glorify You.

Spiritual Challenge

With this lesson on bees, I also challenge you to hold your stingers if people are threatening your world. Don't lash out at them. Give them the honey you produce and the sweetness that comes from God. Try not to sting when you get hurt. Instead of defending yourself, you might just get hurt even worse.

Notes

Donut Shop

Life is like a donut shop that is open 24/7. (This might sound odd, but bear with me.)

When I was young, I had a fear of nighttime. I was afraid there would be an unexpected crisis and no one would be awake to take care of the emergency. I got back to sleep by picturing stores that were open all night. The one store I knew that was open was the 24-hour donut shop down the street. For some odd reason, I felt safe knowing someone in the neighborhood was awake and alert.

Fast forward to college. I continued to fear nighttime, but for a different reason. It meant that I had to get all my studying and homework done before the next day. My roommate and I once had so much work that we decided to pull an all-nighter to get everything done. We told ourselves that if we got through the night productively, we would treat ourselves to the best donuts around. There was also a popular donut shop down the street from my university that was open 24 hours a day.

What was better than knowing the donut shop was open and waiting for me? Knowing that I had a friend who was there for me as well! An encouraging and supportive community is so important. We were created to be in community with one another.

When the world gets dark, and when you feel like you are scared and alone, remember that you are safe with God and that people love you. The people who love me are with me through even tougher tragedies than homework.

When you have lost hope and feel as though no one loves you, remember that Jesus loves you. Then think really hard about someone in your life who truly cares about you, and hold onto that for one more night. Hold onto that through the darkness.

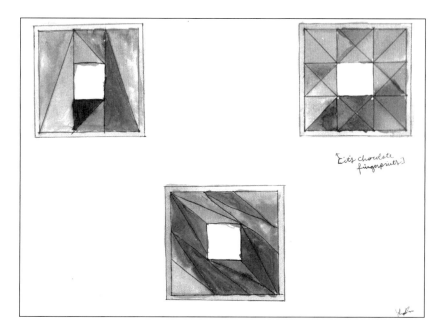

Verses

"And let us consider how we may spur one another on toward love and good deeds, not giving up meeting together, as some are in the habit of doing, but encouraging one another—and all the more as you see the Day approaching." —Hebrews 10:24-25 (NIV)

"For his anger lasts only a moment, but his favor lasts a lifetime; weeping may stay for the night, but rejoicing comes in the morning."
—*Psalm 30:5 (NIV)*

Prayer

Dear Heavenly Father, thank You for the amazing community of people that are in my life. I pray that we would grow together as a community in love and service to You. Help me to fully feel and truly understand that I am loved.

Spiritual Challenge

If you are feeling alone, reach out to someone you trust and grab donuts with them (or whatever treat you like). Be honest and open about how you are feeling, and don't be afraid to ask for prayer. Sometimes it helps me to try and make someone smile if I am going through a difficult time. Seeing joy is infectious and makes me joyful. If you are feeling really brave, show the love of Christ to someone random. The cashier in the store, someone walking their dog—whoever you feel needs some love. It doesn't have to be a grand gesture; sometimes a smile and hello can make all the difference in someone's day.

Notes

_____

_____

_____

_____

_____

_____

_____

_____

_____

_____

_____

_____

_____

_____

_____

_____

_____

_____

Lifesaver

Unfortunately, some people in life are going to try to tear you down. They are going to try to metaphorically drown you, most likely because they are hurt themselves. Instead of letting hurt people bring you down, find the people in life who will help you rise above. The people who are willing to help you out and keep you afloat. Let them be your lifesavers in the sea of sorrow.

It's comfortable, especially if you are an introvert, to hide away and be on an island by yourself. It is easy to avoid people altogether to prevent yourself from getting hurt, but we can become isolated if we do so. God challenges us to step outside of our comfort zones, and that may mean we need to dive deep into the unknown sea and engage with people. The people in our lives will either help us as the lifesavers we need, or they will drag us down further in life.

A person's true character will show through in tough experiences. Friends who truly want what is best for your soul will support you through the difficult times, and even the times of success. Hold onto those people who stand by you. Learn to forgive the people who end up hurting you, because bitterness rots the bones. We are flawed humans, and imperfection is in our nature, but remember above all: God won't let us down. He provides people on our path to help us through the difficult moments.

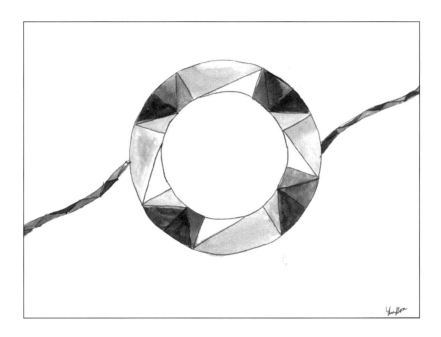

Verses

"As iron sharpens iron, so one person sharpens another."
—*Proverbs 27:17 (NIV)*

"A heart at peace gives life to the body, but envy rots the bones."
—*Proverbs 14:30 (NIV)*

"One who has unreliable friends soon comes to ruin,
but there is a friend who sticks closer than a brother."
—*Proverbs 18:24 (NIV)*

Prayer

Father God, surround me with people who will help me through difficult times. I pray for a strong community of people who care about each other and who desire to lift each other up and grow toward You. Thank You for the people You have placed in my life.

Spiritual Challenge

I challenge you to reach out and connect with someone you know. Spend some quality time with him. Ask him how his soul is doing. You never know when your friends might be going through something.

Notes

Confrontation is like brewing tea. I have been known to be a pas-sive-aggressive person. Admittedly, I can be the type of person who allows people to slight me, lets it bottle up, and then explodes.

My actions can be compared to a tea kettle. The water starts off a slow simmer, but then boils over. The kettle can whistle, which is what I think of when people are so fed up with others they yell at them. And if you let the water boil forever, it will evaporate and you'll be left empty.

You can turn the kettle off and still have hot water, then turn the stove on again and get the water back to a boil. Then off again, therefore never really resolving any issues. Just reheating the same problems with people.

The ideal situation would be to respond to offenses and confi-dently address people with truth and grace. Brew some tea. Make something good out of the confrontation.

If you let the tea bag steep too long, it becomes bitter. If you take it out too fast, the tea is weak. How can we brew the best possible cup of tea and confront people properly? Address them with truth and grace.

My pastor once told me that it is important to give people grace, but also truth. I sometimes identify as a people pleaser, and I often extend a lot of grace for people who have hurt me. But I need to extend truth as well to complement that grace. Too much truth at one time hurts people. Too much grace at one time hurts yourself. We don't want weak tea or bitter tea, so how do we obtain the perfect cup of tea when addressing people?

We can look in the Bible at the story of the adulterous woman who was about to be stoned. In John 8, Jesus instructed the crowd to let the person without sin be the first to throw a stone. No one could do so. Jesus then confronted the woman with truth and grace.

> *"Jesus said, 'Neither do I condemn you; go,*
> *and from now on sin no more.'"–John 8:11 (ESV)*

When you are confronting people, make sure to check your heart and come from a place of love. To take a hurtful situation and make it a positive opportunity to strengthen the relationship is like brewing tea. Make sure to address your friend with truth and grace.

With that being said, sometimes people don't like tea—that is, they aren't interested in making peace. All you can do is enter the

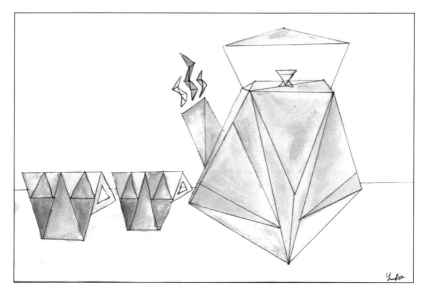

situation with a good heart, and from there the other person will either take it or leave it. If they don't accept your cup of truth and grace, find peace in the fact that you modeled Christ's love for others.

Verses

"Let your conversation be always full of grace, seasoned with salt, so that you may know how to answer everyone." —Colossians 4:6 (NIV)

"Therefore each of you must put off falsehood and speak truthfully to your neighbor, for we are all members of one body. 'In your anger do not sin': Do not let the sun go down while you are still angry, and do not give the devil a foothold. Anyone who has been stealing must steal no longer, but must work, doing something useful with their own hands, that they may have something to share with those in need. Do not let any unwholesome talk come out of your mouths, but only what is helpful for building others up according to their needs, that it may benefit those who listen." —Ephesians 4:25–29 (NIV)

Prayer

Father God, thank You for extending mercy to me. I pray that I would be able to extend that mercy to others. Help me to confront people with biblical truth and grace. Please guard my heart and give me the proper words to say.

Spiritual Challenge

Practice extending truth and grace to someone you are having a difficult time loving.

(Give them some tea!)

Notes

_____

_____

_____

_____

_____

_____

_____

_____

_____

_____

_____

_____

_____

_____

_____

_____

_____

Wind Chime

Be vulnerable and express yourself boldly and elegantly like a wind chime. Share your story and testimony. Wind chimes allow us to know the wind surrounding us is moving in our lives. They let us know that the wind is there and present. Now, we can feel the wind when it touches our skin or pushes our hair, but a wind chime makes wind tangible through more of our senses. Now we can see and hear the effects of the wind.

I believe it is important to share your story. It helps people see how God is moving in your life, and it helps us hear what He has to say through you.

At church one day, I was able to share a part of my testimony. I was so desperate for my family to be united after suffering many losses in my life, and I asked God to work in our lives. When I shared how God was slowly working on uniting my family, one of the band members of the worship team came up to me and shared how he was going through a similar situation with his family. God's work in my life gave this guy hope for his! I felt honored to be able to pass on hope to someone I didn't even know needed it!

I encourage you to share your testimony. Your pain will be relieved a bit, and you might be able to help someone in need! The wind comes and goes, but it cannot be ignored when the sounds of wind chimes echo loudly.

God is so good!

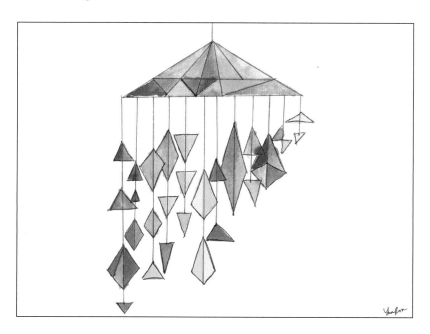

Verses

*Carry each other's burdens, and in this way you will
fulfill the law of Christ. —Galatians 6:2 (NIV)*

*I will come down and speak with you there, and I will take
some of the power of the Spirit that is on you and put it on them.
They will share the burden of the people with you so that you will
not have to carry it alone. —Numbers 11:17 (NIV)*

Prayer

Dear Heavenly Father, I pray that You would use my story to help others. Give me the boldness to share how You have worked in my life. I thank You for the amazing story that You are writing in my life.

Spiritual Challenge

I challenge you to think about your testimony and reflect on how God has worked in your life. Be ready to share it! Your story is powerful! You could also ask someone to share their testimony. It would give someone a chance to let their story be heard.

Notes

For Embracing God's Creative Process and Plan

Part 4

Mountain

Mountains are a great analogy for obstacles in life. Climbing a mountain requires incredible strength and stamina; if you can persevere, triumph and glory are waiting at the top. And the view from the peak will allow you to reflect on how far you have come. All of that is commendable. But what I would like to further discuss is how a mountain can be representative of our dreams, goals, and callings in life.

I am a dreamer. God designed me to be creative. I have a plethora of ideas and projects I would like to create, but I tend to lose focus. I want to climb several mountains at a time, which is impossible; I should focus on one. I tend to start a dream, to metaphorically climb a mountain, but it gets difficult. It gets boring. I get discouraged. I trip and fall. I am tempted to quit.

With the fear of failing and falling, I go back down and attempt to climb a different mountain. I chase a different goal or dream only to trip again, fall again, and go back down the mountain to start something else altogether.

I'm often tempted to quit halfway, to refuse to fully commit to my journey. I am reminded of the Israelites who lacked resolve and never stepped into the Promised Land.

It is not that I haven't ever completed a goal in my life or climbed a metaphorical mountain fully. I just tend to get discouraged a lot. Even writing this devotional has proven to be a mountain. I press on, though, just as God commanded the Israelites to do.

I encourage you to keep going as well. Jesus will be your trekking buddy along the way. Ask Him to help you with your journey. He will prompt you to follow through on your callings in life.

When you climb up a mountain, the pressure gets heavier and it gets harder to breathe. In the same way, as soon as you start following your dreams, pressure builds. You need to make sure you have God's Word breathing life into you as you climb on.

Verses

"Be strong and courageous. Do not be afraid or terrified because of them, for the Lord your God goes with you; he will never leave you nor forsake you." —Deuteronomy 31:6 (NIV)

"You have made your way around this hill country long enough; now turn north." —Deuteronomy 2:3 (NIV)

Prayer

Dear Heavenly Father, thank You for the dreams and callings You have placed in my life. May I continue to lean on You in this journey. Help me to diligently work towards what You have called me to do. Please give me strength, courage, and endurance to press onward. Thank You, Jesus.

Spiritual Challenge

If you are stuck working on something, first turn to God. Seek Him, whether by reading Scripture, praying, or singing worship songs—whatever draws you toward Him. Then I challenge you to take **one step** forward toward your dream, goal, or calling. Some people might take twelve after reading this, but if you are struggling to move at all, just take one step! Sometimes for me, one step meant writing one sentence on a page. I believe in you, but more importantly, God believes in you!

Notes

_____

_____

_____

_____

_____

_____

_____

_____

_____

_____

_____

_____

_____

_____

_____

_____

Hot-Air Balloon

I enjoy journaling and writing. It is how I communicate. Now, some people assume that everything I write is insightful and eloquent, but truth be told, this isn't the case. There are times when I get extremely frustrated and just can't figure out what to write, so a bunch of expletives get written down instead. Then scribbled out, of course.

I also write down a lot of simple sentences like, "I ate a bowl of soup today." Getting those thoughts out allows me to build up to something better. It is like filling a hot-air balloon with air. The mundane sentences get me through and eventually lift me up to grant me a new perspective on situations.

The mundane work we do is important because it prepares us for the journey ahead. If you are questioning why you are in a certain place in life, do not fret. You won't be there forever. If you can, change your perspective to see that God is working in you and through you during this quiet time. You will be lifted up to a new adventure, but in His timing.

If you try to fly a hot-air balloon when it isn't fully inflated, then it won't get very high. God knows what He is doing. He knows your potential, and He knows how high you can go. Don't get discouraged!

[I can see my house from here!]

Verses

"Therefore, my dear brothers and sisters, stand firm.
Let nothing move you. Always give yourselves fully to the work
of the Lord, because you know that your labor in the Lord
is not in vain." —1 Corinthians 15:58 (NIV)

"I will exalt you, Lord, for you lifted me out of the depths
and did not let my enemies gloat over me. Lord my God,
I called to you for help, and you healed me."
—Psalm 30:1–2 (NIV)

Prayer

Father God, let me see the beauty of Your creation during mundane times of life. Please reveal to me that You are with me. I pray for patience as I wait for instruction on how to fulfill what You have called me to do in life.

Spiritual Challenge

As you are doing mundane tasks, remember what Jesus did. Not everything He did was a spectacle. He washed His disciples' feet. He was a carpenter before He started His ministry. Jesus slept on a boat. Not everything we do is glamorous, but I challenge you to see the beauty in the everyday tasks that you are doing.

Notes

_____

_____

_____

_____

_____

_____

_____

_____

_____

_____

_____

_____

_____

_____

_____

_____

_____

_____

Puzzle

Life is like a puzzle, but not just any puzzle. It is one of those puzzle boxes from a thrift shop. The puzzle where you don't know if any of the pieces are missing or if some kid placed a puzzle piece from another box into the one you currently have.

God gives us hopes, dreams, and visions of the future just like the completed puzzle-picture on the outside of the box. However, the end result doesn't always match the vision we are given—or at the very least, the journey is nothing like we imagine.

It is a lot of trial and error. Placing pieces in the wrong space, generally seeing the bigger picture, but not quite getting it on the first try. Sometimes in our frustration, we give up. We lose sight of the vision; we lose some of the puzzle pieces. However, we must not give up hope. We must keep going and keep following God's instructions.

Just like two puzzle pieces clicking together, sometimes we just need to be patient and wait for sudden pivotal shifts in our thought process or for situations in our life to click on God's timing.

Above all, God enjoys being in a relationship with us. He desires time together with us. He enjoys solving this puzzle with us!

Verses

"Not only so, but we also glory in our sufferings, because we know that suffering produces perseverance; perseverance, character; and character, hope. And hope does not put us to shame, because God's love has been poured out into our hearts through the Holy Spirit, who has been given to us."—Romans 5:3–5 (NIV)

"But as for you, be strong and do not give up, for your work will be rewarded."—2 Chronicles 15:7 (NIV)

Prayer

Dear Heavenly Father, thank You for all the callings and dreams You have placed in my heart. Please bring them to fruition as I seek to glorify You above all. I ask for patience during discouraging times. I greatly enjoy Your presence and our time together as you put my current circumstances into perspective.

Spiritual Challenge

Are you in the midst of a creative project? Or are you wanting to start one? I challenge you to first ask God for help, and then take one step forward in the creative process. Be open to your surroundings so you don't miss what God has to say. When I ask God for creative input, He usually brings someone into my life with insightful information, or He places a much-needed word of encouragement before me.

Notes

Jump Rope

I remember playing jump rope in elementary school. Timing was everything. My friends and I would enthusiastically run under and jump over the rope. There would be the occasional slap in the face if the rhythm was off or if you charged into the rope at the wrong time—or if someone cynically wanted you to fail. That happened on occasion too. We would purposefully try to trip one another.

Anyway, whenever I get frustrated at *my* timing, I remember that everything is on God's timing. He has something better planned than what I could ever conceive in my head. He's got the rope swinging; we just have to be willing to jump.

There was a time when I was desperately applying for jobs. I heard about an opening with a nonprofit organization that built schools in different countries. Similar to missions trips, but without the faith aspect. I made it to the final interview, but I was ultimately rejected. That stung a little, and I felt discouraged.

However, a few weeks later, the missions organization that I had previously served with contacted me regarding a ministry position! God provided the position on His timing! The job ended up being better than the one I interviewed for because I was able to express my faith at work and I grew a lot from the missions work.

Trust God's timing. He wants what is best for you. We must be patient and trust in Him. It is difficult when you are pressured. The world screams at you, people scream at you, sometimes we scream at ourselves for not being where we think we should be. Despite the frustration, we must trust in the Lord! He wants what is best for you; and at the end of the day, He is the only one that matters.

Verses

"There is a time for everything, and a season for every activity under the heavens." —Ecclesiastes 3:1 (NIV)

"He has made everything beautiful in its time. He has also set eternity in the human heart; yet no one can fathom what God has done from beginning to end." —Ecclesiastes 3:11 (NIV)

"Wait for the Lord; be strong and take heart and wait for the Lord."
—*Psalm 27:14 (NIV)*

Prayer

Dear God, thank You for the many opportunities You have lined up ahead in my life. Help me to listen and wait patiently for Your timing on everything. When You ask me to take a leap of faith, may I have the courage and strength to do so.

Spiritual Challenge

Wait for God's timing and have faith in Him. He wants you to succeed; you just have to practice patience and trust.

Notes

Carnival Game

My father and I were at a carnival walking around the games section. As we walked past the darts game, I saw a little stuffed flower on the table. The flower was actually the consolation prize if you weren't able to hit the middle of the target. I asked my dad if he could play the game so I could get the consolation flower. My dad happily agreed, relieved that I wasn't even thinking about the bigger prizes. I only wanted the small one. He had nothing to lose.

We went up to the counter and my father paid to play. The host of the game handed my father three darts. The first dart was an intentional miss. The second dart was also an intentional miss. The third dart, however, was an unintentional win! My father had accidentally managed to get the dart on the rim of the inner bullseye.

Instead of a small consolation flower, the lady at the counter handed me a huge stuffed beagle. It was the size of me at the time. I remember walking over to the rest of my family with my huge stuffed toy dog. Everyone was shocked.

My new stuffed toy dog was not what I expected at all. It was kind of a nuisance during the ride home because we were all already cramped in the car, and now we had to fit this huge dog in there. Once we got it home, however, that stuffed toy dog was comfy to lay on, and my brothers would lean on it whenever they played video games. The stuffed beagle wasn't what I wanted, but it was even better.

I believe this is how God answers our prayers. Not through the random chance of a dart throw—what I mean is that He does not answer our prayers in the way that we anticipate. But He answers them in a way that is better than we can ever imagine. Pray to God with your whole heart and expect Him to answer. He gives us the desires of our hearts.

Verses

"Take delight in the Lord, and he will give you the desires of your heart." —Psalm 37:4 (NIV)

"Now to him who is able to do immeasurably more than all we ask or imagine, according to his power that is at work within us."
—*Ephesians 3:20 (NIV)*

Prayer

Father God, thank You for always answering my prayers. I confidently go to You with my prayers knowing full well that You have my best interests at heart.

Spiritual Challenge

Boldly ask God for something, and then wait and see how He works in your life!

Notes

Connect-the-Dots Picture

I arrived at a local restaurant with my family. The host asked us if we required any children's menus. Sixteen-year-old me delightfully shouted, "Yes!"

Every once in a while, I like entertaining my inner child.

As I contentedly colored the flimsy paper menu with a half-broken crayon, I noticed there was a connect-the-dots picture. From a quick glance, the picture looked like a random cluster of dots. However, I could see the image would eventually be a flower. Perhaps if I were younger, I wouldn't know the hidden shape from looking at the dots; however, I had meticulously trained my eye to perceive things from a larger scope.

God's elaborate plans for our lives can be similar to a connect-the-dots drawing. Our circumstances or the events that happen to us only make sense when we look at them in reverse or from a broader perspective.

When I was in high school, I begrudgingly took an advanced history class. I earnestly begged my academic counselor to switch me to regular history. She told me every class was full, and I couldn't switch out. It was a grueling year, and I ended up failing my Advanced Placement test at the end of the year.

Even though in that season of life I was miserable, I am so appreciative now. Looking back at the situation, it was a blessing in disguise.

Because I didn't pass my requisite Advanced Placement test, I needed to take a course in college that satisfied the specific requirement. And I had the opportunity to fulfill the requirement during my academic semester studying near Yosemite! What a huge blessing to study humanities in divine nature! If I had previously passed my test, I would never have been placed on the path to spend a semester in the mountains.

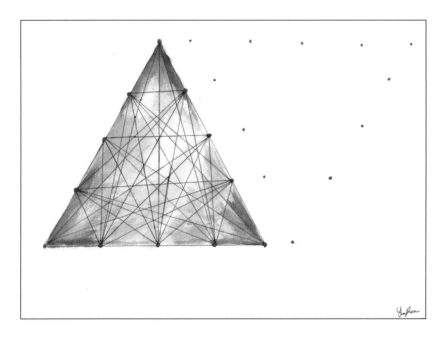

Another tremendous blessing that sprouted from my AP failure was our year-end class project. Our teacher assigned us to record an interview with someone from our family and create a scrapbook in honor of their history. I chose to interview my grandma. There was a slight language barrier between us, so I interviewed my father in a supplement to my grandma's interview. They both had compelling stories and life lessons from living in the Philippines. My father and grandma both passed away a few years later, but I have precious recordings from each of them.

Even though I strongly detested the history class at the moment, I am able to see that God used my apparent failure and crafted it into something beautiful. For that, I am thankful.

If you are in a season of apparent distress, have faith because God will turn negative experiences into something beautiful. You just have to wait to see the bigger picture.

Verses

"However, as it is written: 'What no eye has seen, what no ear has heard, and what no human mind has conceived'– the things God has prepared for those who love him–"–1 Corinthians 2:9 (NIV)

"The Lord will work out his plans for my life– for your faithful love, O Lord, endures forever. Don't abandon me, for you made me."
—Psalm 138:8 (NLT)

"The Lord himself goes before you and will be with you; he will never leave you nor forsake you. Do not be afraid; do not be discouraged." —Deuteronomy 31:8 (NIV)

Prayer

Dear God, even though I cannot see the future, I trust that You are carefully crafting something great for me. Please take my confusion and pain and turn it into something beautiful. Thank You in advance for the wonderful story You are already working on through me.

Spiritual Challenge

Reflect and think of a time in the past when you knew God had worked together something good. Memories like this can remind you that God does continuously work in your life. If you are in a season of doubt, remembering God's faithfulness can help you hold onto hope in the future.

Notes

Egg Hunt

I love Easter. There's the obvious reason of Jesus' resurrection, but I also love Easter because of the Easter egg hunts my mom would send us on as a kid. This was no ordinary egg hunt with eggs just thrown everywhere. No, my mom carefully, meticulously, and creatively wrote a riddle for each egg. One leading to another.

In the same way, God teaches us and leads us along each step of the journey of life. We shouldn't always fixate on the end goal. Yes, that is important, but He wants to help us and guide us along the way.

My mom would hand us the beginning clue, which would tell us where to find an egg. We would have to carefully read the note and really think about what she was trying to say. It was fun!

Similarly, God doesn't always reveal His plans to us plainly. This is not out of spite, but so we may enjoy the journey! He may not give us plain instruction, but neither does He abandon us to figure it out totally on our own. He is with us and guiding us along the way. My mom would never leave us and be like, "Alright, I'm going to go away now." No! She wanted to witness and be a part of our journey! God does not want to leave us behind; He wants to be with us!

He is going to help us during tough times and give us little pieces of help amidst the chaos.

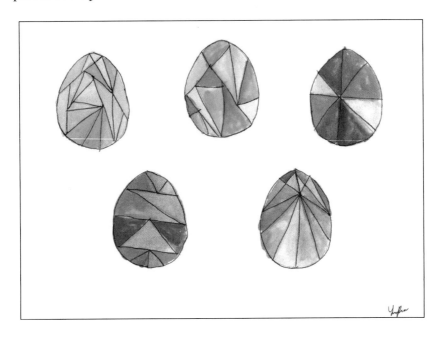

Verses

"But seek first his kingdom and his righteousness, and all these things will be given to you as well."—Matthew 6:33 (NIV)

"And without faith it is impossible to please God, because anyone who comes to him must believe that he exists and that he rewards those who earnestly seek him." —Hebrews 11:6 (NIV)

"I will instruct you and teach you in the way you should go; I will counsel you with my loving eye on you." —Psalm 32:8 (NIV)

Prayer

Dear God, thank You for sending me on a fun journey of life. May I be able to hear You and seek You always.

Spiritual Challenge

Think of how God has helped you along the way in life, and continuously ask Him to guide you. Look for God's "hints" every day!

Notes

_____

_____

_____

_____

_____

_____

_____

_____

_____

_____

_____

_____

_____

_____

_____

_____

_____

Stage

When I was a kid, I was in a community theater group. I remember standing in the wings quietly waiting to go on stage during a scene change. The lights were dim and the stage crew was assembling the next scene practically in the dark. The scene transition was so

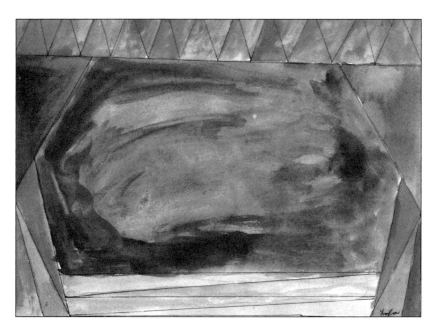

smooth; the point was to make sure the audience didn't get distracted from the musical or play happening before them.

I believe this is how God works. Whenever I am frustrated that I can't see anything, whenever I'm in a dark time, I remind myself God is on my side, and He is working on my behalf to set the stage on which I will perform for His glory. I just have to patiently wait in the wings for His cue.

I believe my calling in life is to start a creative arts nonprofit, and I get so frustrated that I can't see what God is doing in front of me on my behalf. I must trust in Him and have faith that He is already working on every detail. I just have to wait for His timing on everything.

Verses

"And we know that in all things God works for the good of those who love him, who have been called according to his purpose."
—Romans 8:28 (NIV)

"The Lord is good to those whose hope is in him, to the one who seeks him; it is good to wait quietly for the salvation of the Lord."
—Lamentations 3:25-26 (NIV)

"We have this hope as an anchor for the soul, firm and secure. It enters the inner sanctuary behind the curtain." —Hebrews 6:19 (NIV)

Prayer

Father God, thank You for arranging everything on my behalf. I pray that I may have patience while I wait for Your instruction. Let me see life from a larger scope, and let my faith carry me through the unknown.

Spiritual Challenge

I challenge you to meditate on God's Word. You could also pray and listen to worship music. Just practice being still today.

Notes

Closing Remarks

Thank you so much for reading these analogies all the way through. I hope it was encouraging (and semi-entertaining) to read. I know these devotionals are a bit unconventional, but my hope is that it sparked something inside you to go out and live. Live for God.

Life gets difficult. It gets dreary, dull, and just plain awful. I hope to encourage you to find ways for your soul to be refreshed. When we are filled and inspired, we are able to go out into the world and help others.

I understand though that it is tough. We don't always feel effective. That is okay! We are loved by our Creator no matter what. I fully believe we were each crafted for a purpose. Love sustains us, and inspiration fuels us forward. It does for me, anyway.

I just hope to show you that it does not take a perfect person or perfect circumstances to be effective and influential in the world. We all have the capability to influence those around us. If you're up for it, allow God to work in your heart and soul to reveal your purpose in the world. I believe creating is a form of faith; so, my dear, go out and create!

Made in the USA
Monee, IL
18 May 2020